God Shows Us His Love

Twelve Bible Stories for Young Children

Book One

 Authors: Lynn Groth and Ellen Hinz
Illustrator: Kate Endle
Third printing, 2011
Second printing, 2004

© 1999 Northwestern Publishing House. All rights reserved.

**Northwestern Publishing House
Milwaukee, WI**

God Made All Things

Genesis 1

In the beginning, long ago, there was only God. There was no world. There were no people, animals, plants, or lakes.

God said, "I will make a world." God did not use a hammer and nails or paper and tape as people do when they make things. God used just his power and his words to make everything. He took six days to make the world.

> Day 1: God made the day, and God made the night.
> He looked, and everything was right.
>
> Day 2: God spoke from his home on high,
> And with his power he made a sky.
>
> Day 3: God made lakes and hills and sand.
> He made plants grow on the land.
>
> Day 4: God made the moon; God made the sun.
> He made the stars, yes, every one.
>
> Day 5: God made birds with wings and tails.
> God made fish and sharks and whales.
>
> Day 6: God made animals on the land.
> God made people, far more grand!

The first two people were a man named Adam and a woman named Eve. God looked at the wonderful world he had made. It was very good! It was just what God wanted. God said, "My world is now done." On day 7 God did not make anything else, but he kept watching over his wonderful world.

Prayer
Thanks, dear God, for the great big world,
For each animal, star, and tree.
Thanks for the rivers, hills, and sky;
And thanks, dear God, for making me! Amen.

Story One See page 27 for activities to do with your child.

God's Plan to Save People

Genesis 2 and 3

God made a wonderful world. He made Adam and Eve, the first two people. God also made a beautiful garden. God told Adam and Eve, "This garden is for you. It is your happy home. You may eat fruit from every tree but one." God told them which tree they should never eat from. He wanted them to listen to what he said and not eat from that tree. Adam and Eve loved God and did what he said.

But one day a snake talked to Eve. The devil made the snake talk. The devil does not want people to love and obey God. The snake said, "Eat this good fruit, Eve."

Eve ate the forbidden fruit. Then she gave some to Adam, and he ate it too. They did not listen to God. They listened to the devil. They sinned.

Adam and Eve knew they had done something wrong. They tried to hide from God. But God knew where they were. He said, "I will send someone to help you. He will fight the devil and win." God promised to send Jesus to take away all the wrong things people do.

God told Adam and Eve, "You have sinned. You will not be happy all the time anymore."

Adam and Eve knew that someday they would die because they had sinned. But they also knew that God loved them. He would take their sins away and give them life in heaven. God would do all this through Jesus.

Prayer
Jesus, I am sorry for every sin I do.
Please take away my sins, and help me live for you. Amen.

Story Two See pages 27 and 28 for activities to do with your child.

God Saves Noah and His Family

Genesis 6–9:17

God was good to Adam and Eve and gave them children. Those children grew up and had more children. Soon the world was full of people. But all the people were sinners. They did not always love and obey God.

Only one family still believed in God. There was Noah and his wife. They had three sons. Each son had a wife. They all believed in God and his promise to take away their sins. But all the other people in the world did not believe in God. They did not listen to God. They loved to do bad things.

One day God said, "Noah, I am going to send lots of rain. There will be a flood. There will be so much water that the people and animals on the land will die." Then God said, "Build a very big boat called an ark. Put food into the ark. Put two of every bird, animal, and creeping bug into the ark. Put your family into the ark. I will save you and your family inside the ark."

Noah loved God and did everything he said to do. Noah and his family got into the ark, and God closed the door.

Then God sent the flood. Water came down from the sky. Water came up from the ground. It rained for 40 days and 40 nights. That's a long time!

The trees and mountains were all covered with water. The people and animals on the land died. But God saved Noah and his family inside the ark.

Then God made the water go down, down. The ark went down, down. Then the ark came to a stop on a mountain. Noah waited until God told him to come out of the ark. Noah, his family, and their animals were safe! They all came out of the ark. Noah and his family thanked God for saving them.

Then God put a rainbow in the sky. He said, "I won't send a flood like this one ever again."

Prayer
Dear God, thank you for the rainbow
Of colors up above.
It tells me of your promise.
It tells me of your love. Amen.

Story Three See page 28 for activities to do with your child.

Jesus Is Born

Luke 2:1-20

A man named Joseph was on his way to a town called Bethlehem. Joseph took his wife, Mary, along. She was going to have a baby very, very soon. An angel had told Mary, "Your baby will be God's Son, Jesus. He will take away the sins of all people."

When Joseph and Mary got to Bethlehem, they were tired. They tried to find a room to stay in, but all the rooms were full. One man told Joseph, "People are already staying in all my rooms. But if you want, you may sleep in my barn."

Joseph and Mary had no other place to go, so they stayed in the stable, a barn. Something very wonderful happened that night. Baby Jesus was born! Mary wrapped Jesus in long strips of cloth. She laid him in a manger, a box used to feed the animals.

God kept his promise. He sent his Son, Jesus, into the world. Jesus grew up and saved people from their sins.

Prayer
Thank you, God, for Jesus,
Born on Christmas Day.
Thank you, God, for Jesus.
He took my sins away. Amen.

Story Four See pages 28 and 29 for activities to do with your child.

The Boy Jesus

Luke 2:41-52

Jesus did not stay a baby. Soon he grew to be a little boy. He learned to walk and talk. Jesus played and ate and slept just as you do. But Jesus was also the Son of God. He did not sin even one time. He always listened to Mary and Joseph and obeyed them. Jesus always did what was right so that he could save us from the wrong things we do.

Jesus loved to learn about God's Word. When Jesus was 12 years old, Mary and Joseph told him, "Now you are old enough to walk with us to a big church called the temple. It is in another city." That made Jesus happy! Jesus walked with his friends and family day after day. It was a long walk! But finally they came to the big temple. Many people were in town to praise God at the big church. Jesus spent his time listening to the teachers talk about God and his Word.

After a few days, it was time to walk back home. Mary and Joseph thought Jesus was walking with their big group of friends and family, but Jesus was still at the temple, listening to God's Word. At night when it was time to sleep, Mary and Joseph looked for Jesus. All the people with them said, "We have not seen Jesus all day."

So Mary and Joseph walked back to the city to look for him. They looked by the houses. They looked on the streets. No Jesus! Finally they looked in the big temple. There he was!

Jesus was with the men who taught God's Word. The teachers said, "This boy really knows a lot about God and his Word!"

Jesus told Mary and Joseph what he was doing while they were gone. He was doing what his Father in heaven wanted him to do. When Mary and Joseph said it was time to go, Jesus went with them. Jesus loved his parents and always obeyed them.

Prayer
Jesus, help me listen to your Word each day.
Jesus, help me love and trust you and obey. Amen.

Story Five See pages 29 and 30 for activities to do with your child.

Jesus Heals a Blind Man

Mark 10:46-52; Luke 18:35-43

Jesus told people God's Word. He told them God had sent him to take away their sins. Sometimes Jesus showed his power by making sick people well.

One day Jesus was walking with a crowd of people. There was a blind man sitting beside the road. People who are blind cannot see. The blind man could not work to earn money, so he would sit by the road and beg people to give him money. When the blind man heard many people walking by, he said, "Tell me what is happening!"

Some people answered, "Jesus is passing by."

This news made the blind man happy. He thought, "I know who Jesus is, and I know he can help me." Then he called out, "Jesus, you are the Savior God promised to send. Please help me!"

Some of the people did not like to hear the blind man shouting, and they told him to be quiet. But the blind man shouted even more, "Jesus, my Savior, please show me your love and help me!"

Jesus heard the man praying for help and said, "Bring that man to me."

People told the blind man, "Be happy! Get up! Jesus wants you to come." The man was happy. He jumped up. Some people led him to Jesus.

"What do you want me to do for you?" Jesus asked the man.

The blind man answered, "Oh, Jesus, please help my eyes so that I can see."

Jesus then said to him, "Yes, I will make your eyes able to see. You believe and trust in me."

Right then the man could see! Jesus had healed his eyes. The man was so happy that he walked along with Jesus and gave him thanks and praise.

Prayer
Thank you for eyes, ears, mouth, and nose.
Thank you for fingers, knees, and toes.
Thank you, Lord God, for making me.
Now help me serve you happily. Amen.

Story Six See page 30 for activities to do with your child.

Jesus Feeds Many, Many People

Portions of Matthew 14, Mark 6, Luke 9, and John 6

Many, many people came to see Jesus one day. There were thousands and thousands of people. Jesus taught God's Word to them and helped the people who were sick get well.

Late in the day the people became hungry, but they had nothing to eat. Jesus asked some of his friends, "Where will we buy food for all these people?" He wanted to see what his friends would say.

One of Jesus' friends said, "Lord, it would take a lot of money to buy food for all these people!"

Another one of Jesus' friends said, "Jesus, there is a boy here who has a lunch. He has five pieces of bread and two small fish. But that cannot feed all these people."

Then Jesus told his friends, "Have all the people sit down." So the friends had all the people sit down on the grass. The ground was covered with people! Then Jesus took the boy's bread and fish and thanked his Father in heaven for the food. Jesus broke the food into pieces and gave some to his friends to pass out to the other people. Each time Jesus' friends gave some food away, there was still more left in their hands! There was plenty of food for everyone!

All the people had plenty to eat. Then Jesus said to his friends, "Now go get all the food that is left. We don't want to waste any of it." Jesus' friends took the food that was left and put it into baskets. The food filled 12 baskets! There was much more food left over than what Jesus had started with!

Jesus had shown his power as the Son of God by making a little lunch feed thousands and thousands of people.

Prayer
Food is tasty, fun to eat,
And it helps me grow.
Thank you, God, for all my food.
You love me, this I know! Amen.

Story Seven See page 31 for activities to do with your child.

Jesus Quiets the Storm

Portions of Matthew 8, Mark 4, and Luke 8

Jesus was teaching his Word to many people near a lake. When the day was over, he told his friends, "Let's get into a boat and sail to the other side of the lake." So Jesus and his friends began to sail across the lake. Jesus was so tired that he fell asleep in the back of the boat.

Suddenly there was a terrible storm! The wind blew. It made big waves on the water. The waves went over the sides of the boat. So much water came into the boat that Jesus' friends were afraid the boat would sink.

The friends woke Jesus up and said, "Lord, save us! We are going to drown!"

Jesus told his friends, "Why are you so afraid? Why don't you trust in me?" Then Jesus got up and spoke to the wind and the waves. He told the storm, "Quiet! Be still!" Right away the storm stopped. The wind quieted down, and the big waves were gone.

Jesus told his friends, "Have faith in me to help you."

The friends were amazed at the power Jesus had. They said, "Even the wind and the waves do what Jesus says!"

Prayer
Jesus, storms are sometimes scary,
But I know you're everywhere.
You are watching me and helping.
Thank you, Jesus, for you care. Amen.

Story Eight See pages 31 and 32 for activities to do with your child.

People Praise Jesus as Their King

Portions of Matthew 21, Mark 11, Luke 19, and John 12

Jesus was on his way to the city of Jerusalem. He knew what would happen there. He would die on a cross to take away the sins of all people. But first he would ride into the city as a king.

Jesus had some of his friends go and get him a little donkey to ride. They put their coats on the donkey's back. Then Jesus sat on the donkey and rode into the city.

Many people came to see Jesus. Some walked in front of him. Some walked behind him. Many of the people put their coats on the road for the donkey to walk on. Others cut branches from palm trees. They laid the branches down on the road with the coats.

The people were very happy to see Jesus! They praised Jesus and shouted, "Hosanna!" *Hosanna* means, "Save (us)!" Over and over again people said, "Hosanna! Praise to Jesus! He is the Savior God promised to send. Hosanna! Blessed is the King who comes in the name of the Lord!" How happy the people were to give praise to Jesus!

Prayer

Jesus, I love you!
Jesus, I praise you!
Help me obey you
In all that I do. Amen.

Story Nine See page 32 for activities to do with your child.

Jesus Dies for All People

Portions of Matthew 27, Mark 15, Luke 23, and John 19

Many people loved Jesus. But many others did not love him. The people who did not love Jesus said, "He should die. Let's get rid of Jesus!"

Some men took Jesus and put him on a wooden cross to die. They nailed his hands to the cross. They nailed his feet to the cross. Then they left Jesus hanging there to die. This hurt Jesus very, very much.

Jesus hung on the cross all morning. He was still there in the afternoon. Some people laughed at him and said, "Jesus, if you really are the Son of God, come down from the cross." Jesus could have come down from the cross, but he stayed on it. He wanted to die to take away the sins of all people.

It was daytime, but suddenly the sky became very dark. God made it dark. Jesus was suffering very much, even though he had done nothing wrong. Then Jesus cried out, "It is finished!" and died. Jesus was done with his work of taking away the sins of all people. Oh, how much Jesus loves us!

Prayer
Jesus, I am sorry
For all the wrong I do.
I thank you that you died for me.
Please help me live for you. Amen.

Story Ten See pages 32 and 33 for activities to do with your child.

Jesus Is Alive!

Portions of Matthew 28, Mark 16, Luke 24, and John 20

Jesus had died on the cross. He let this happen to him. He wanted to take away the sins of all people.

Two friends of Jesus took his body down from the cross. They laid his dead body in a little cave called a tomb. A tomb is a little room where dead people were put. The friends left Jesus' body inside the tomb and rolled a big stone in front of the doorway. Then they walked away sadly. Jesus was dead.

For one, two, three days, Jesus was dead in the tomb. But on the morning of day 3, a very wonderful thing happened. Jesus came back to life! He came right out of the tomb. He did not even need to roll away the big stone.

Some other special things also happened when Jesus rose from the dead. The ground shook. An angel came down from heaven. He rolled the stone away from the tomb. The angel was as bright as lightning.

Some women came to the tomb that morning. They were afraid to see an angel there. But the angel told them, "Don't be afraid. You're looking for Jesus, aren't you? Well, he is not here. He has come back from the dead as he said he would. Go and tell Jesus' friends that he is alive."

The women were very happy to hear this news! They ran to share this news with others. Suddenly Jesus met them. "Hello!" he said. "Don't be afraid. Go tell my friends that I am alive." The women listened to Jesus. They went to tell his friends right away. How good it was to see Jesus alive again!

Prayer
"Jesus rose! He is alive!"
The shining angel said.
Lord Jesus, I'm so happy
That you rose from the dead. Amen.

Story Eleven See page 33 for activities to do with your child.

Jesus Goes Back to Heaven

Portions of Matthew 28, Luke 24, and Acts 1

After Jesus rose from the dead, he spent many days with his friends. He told them more about God's Word. Jesus told them, "Go out into the world and tell other people what I have done. Tell them that I died to take away all sins. Tell them that I came back to life. I am the Son of God, and I have all power. I will help you as you teach others about me. Remember, I am always with you."

Then one day Jesus told his friends to meet him on a hill near a little town. Jesus told his friends, "I am going to send God the Holy Spirit to you. He will help you be strong and brave as you tell others about me." Jesus put his hands up and blessed his friends. Suddenly Jesus' feet were not on the ground anymore! Jesus began to go up into the sky, higher and higher. Then a cloud covered Jesus. The friends kept looking up, but they could not see Jesus any longer. He had gone back to heaven.

Suddenly two angels stood next to Jesus' friends. The angels said, "Why are you standing here, looking into the sky? Jesus has gone back to heaven. But he will come back through the clouds someday."

Then the friends went to the city of Jerusalem. Each day they prayed to the Lord and gave him praise. They were happy to know that Jesus was with them, even though they could not see him.

Prayer
Jesus, I know you're in heaven.
But you're also with me every day.
I trust you and love you, dear Jesus.
Please watch as I sleep, work, or play. Amen.

Story Twelve See page 34 for activities to do with your child.

Look and See

Lynn Groth

1. Look and see what God has done for me! He made the sun shine in the sky. He made the birds that fly up high. He made the dogs with wag-ging tails. He made the fish, the sharks, the whales. Look and see what God has done for me!

2. Look and see what God has done for me! He gave me his own spe-cial book. It is the Bib-le; take a look! It tells how Je-sus took a-way the sin-ful things I do each day. Look and see what God has done for me!

Text, Tune, Setting: © 1999 Northwestern Publishing House.

Activities

Story One

1. Help your child make a creation place mat. Divide a sheet of paper into six equal boxes. Make the first box half dark and half white. Your child will color the white part yellow to represent light (day). Make a cloud in box 2; grass and a flower in box 3; the sun, moon, and stars in box 4; fish and birds in box 5; and land animals and the faces of a man and woman in box 6. Make all the pictures simple to color. Talk about each picture as your child colors it.

   Variation: Cover the place mat with clear adhesive paper. Then your child may color it with wipe-off crayons or markers.

2. Gather toy animals, birds, fish, trees, and two people to represent Adam and Eve. Help your child draw land, water, and sky on a large sheet of paper. Set the paper on the floor and set each toy in the place it would live or travel.

3. Draw each of the numbers 1 to 6 on its own index card or sheet of paper. Show the numbers in order as you read the six short rhymes in the story. After a while your child may be able to show the appropriate number for each day.

4. As you and your child go for walks and talk about the things God made, carry a garbage bag. Pick up litter, reminding your child that God wants us to take care of his beautiful world.

Story Two

1. Have your child use chalk to draw sad faces on the sidewalk. Wash the pictures away completely with water. This reminds us that God takes our sins away completely through Jesus' death and resurrection.

2. Teach your child the following song by singing the words to the tune of "The Farmer in the Dell." Then add the actions. You may sing the song while doing Activity 1. If your child has washable crayons to use in the bathtub, sing the song while washing away the crayon marks!

   My sins are washed away.
   (pretend to scrub)

   My sins are washed away.
   (pretend to scrub)

   Jesus took away my sins.
   (form cross with arms)

   My sins are washed away.
   (pretend to scrub)

3. Help your child make a tree, snake, and cross from clay. Talk about how the devil came as a snake and told Eve to sin by eating from the tree. Then talk about the Savior that God promised to send. That Savior was Jesus, who died on the cross to take sins away. Point to the cross. Then crush the snake and tell your child that Jesus won against the devil and will take us to heaven someday.

Story Three

1. Tape sheets of colored paper together in this order: red, orange, yellow, green, blue, purple. Lay them on the floor. Help your child set toys on the colored papers, sorting them by color.

    Variation: Staple the sheets into a book. Help your child cut colorful items from old magazines and glue them to the matching pages.

2. Hang a prism in a window to create bands of colors on the walls of your home.

3. Teach the following words and actions to your child:

    A boat saved Noah from the flood,
    (cup hands to form boat)

    But Jesus saves from sin.
    (point up)

    He died upon a cross for me.
    (form cross with arms)

    I trust and follow him.
    (press hands on heart)

    I trust and follow him.
    (press hands on heart)

4. Have your child take some play animals and climb inside a box. Cover the box with a sheet or towel. Have your child pretend to be Noah inside the ark. Shake the "ark" as you say, "Noah, Noah, are you safe inside the ark?" Then have your child lift the lid and say, "Yes, Lord, yes, Lord, I am safe inside the ark."

Story Four

1. Purchase or make a child-proof nativity set so that your child can act out the Christmas account. Homemade sets can be made from paper or clay or by gluing pictures to blocks of wood. Christmas cards may provide pictures of Mary, Joseph, baby Jesus, and some animals.

2. On December 1, you could begin a countdown to Christmas Day. Here are two suggestions:

    - Make 25 paper strips (1" x 8") from red and green paper. Make a paper chain and hang it in your home. Help your child cut off one link each day until December 25.

- Color a small jewelry box brown. This is a manger. Fill a sack with 25 pieces of straw or strips of yellow paper. Have your child take out one piece of straw or paper each day and set it in the manger. On December 25, place the last piece of straw and add a small baby doll or one you have made from paper or clay.

3. Teach your child the following words to the tune of "Twinkle, Twinkle, Little Star."

    Christmas is the Savior's birth.
    Jesus came from heaven to earth.
    Jesus came to take away
    All the sins we do each day.
    Christmas is the Savior's birth.
    Jesus came from heaven to earth.

Story Five

1. Collect the following items for acting out the Bible lesson: toy people, sheets of paper folded into tents, and a box for the temple. Help your child move the people; have them camp, walk, camp; and then bring them to the temple. Place Jesus and some teachers outside the temple, talking. Priests went inside the temple; others met in the outer courtyard. Then have Mary, Joseph, and other people leave. Bring Mary and Joseph back to find Jesus, and then take them all home.

2. Teach your child the following finger play:

    Five little friends came to my house to play.
    (show fingers and thumb)

    The first one said, "I went to church today!"
    (wiggle thumb)

    The second one said, "I heard about God's love."
    (wiggle index finger)

    The third one said, "God lives in heaven above."
    (wiggle middle finger)

    The fourth one said, "In church I sang a song."
    (wiggle ring finger)

    The fifth one said, "I took a friend along!"
    (wiggle pinkie finger)

    The five little friends were happy that they knew
    (wiggle all fingers and thumb)

    The good news of God's love for me and for you!
    (point to self, and then out)

3. Sing the following words to the tune of "The Mulberry Bush." Encourage your child to create actions for each verse.

> This is the way we dress for church, dress for church,
>   dress for church.
> This is the way we dress for church
> On a Sunday morning.

Additional verses: drive to church, walk to church, listen in church, sing in church, pray in church.

Story Six

1. Teach the following song to the tune of "The Farmer in the Dell." Also try the actions. After your child knows the song, try stanza 2. You and your child can add the name of something you see.

> Oh, I have eyes to see.
> *(point to eyes)*
>
> Oh, I have eyes to see.
> *(point to eyes)*
>
> Oh, I have eyes to see the world.
> *(motion in a circle with hand)*
>
> God gave these eyes to me.
> *(point up)*
>
> Oh, I can see the _____.
> *(point to object named)*
>
> Oh, I can see the _____.
> Oh, I have eyes to see the _____.
> God gave these eyes to me.
> *(point up)*

2. Act out the story with your child. Take turns being blindfolded and pretending to be the blind man. Talk to each other as Jesus and the blind man spoke in the story. Then have "Jesus" take the blindfold off so the "blind man" can see.

3. Make a "touch box." Cut a hole in the side of a box so that your child's hand can fit through it. Place two or three familiar objects inside the box. Have your child feel the objects and guess what they are. Then remove the objects to look at them. Thank God for the wonderful gift of sight!

4. Look at a family photo album. Cover the photos with a black sheet of paper. This is similar to what people see when they are blind—no people, just darkness. Praise God for healthy eyes that can see photos and the people we love!

5. Clip a small piece of sponge to a spring-action clothespin. Let your child dab the sponge into paint and make a design. God gives us pretty colors and patterns to see and enjoy.

Story Seven

1. Talk with your child about the various foods that come from milk: cheese, yogurt, ice cream, and so on. Talk about where fruits and vegetables grow: on trees, under the ground, on bushes, on vines.

2. Teach your child the following words to the tune of "Twinkle, Twinkle, Little Star." Add the actions, if you wish.

    Way down under in the ground
    (crouch low)
    Grow potatoes, nice and round.

    Apples, peaches grow on trees;
    (stand with arms out like branches)
    And in gardens—lettuce, peas.

    God has blessed us from above.
    Thank him for his gifts and love.
    (fold hands)

3. To help your child better understand Jesus' miracle, try the following idea. Take a cracker. Break it into pieces and give one to each member of the family and to your child's action figures or dolls. Eventually you will run out, and no one will be full. Jesus used a small lunch to satisfy the hunger of thousands of people. That was a miracle!

4. When you want your child to try a new food, be sure you also serve many favorites. Children who see foods they like know they will not go hungry! Encourage your child to try at least a little of a new food.

5. Give your child a paper plate and some clay. Encourage your child to shape the clay in the form of a favorite meal.

Story Eight

1. Teach your child the following words to the tune of "He's Got the Whole World in His Hands."

    Lord Jesus, you have the world . . . in your hands.
    Lord Jesus, you have the world . . . in your hands.
    Lord Jesus, you have the world . . . in your hands.
    You have the whole world in your hands.

    You told the wind and the waves . . . "Peace. Be still!"
    You told the wind and the waves . . . "Peace. Be still!"
    You told the wind and the waves . . . "Peace. Be still!"
    You have the whole world in your hands.

2. Record real storm sounds or record storm sounds made by you and your child (wind, thunder). Play the sounds back as you retell the story.

3. Explain to your child what to do when there is a storm. Practice safety procedures. Teach your child the prayer given with this Bible story, and pray it together during storms.

4. Make tiny boats by cutting 1-inch sections from the bottom of Styrofoam cups. Put clay into the cups. Glue a paper sail to a toothpick, and press one end of the toothpick into the clay. Sail the boats, and make waves with your hand as you act out the story.

5. Use colorful cloth, crepe paper, ric rac, ribbon, wrapping paper, or tissue paper to make long streamers. Tape or glue them to the end of a cardboard tube. Have your child wave the streamers and blow like a strong wind!

Story Nine

1. Teach your child the following words to the tune of "The Farmer in the Dell." After your child knows the song, substitute *clap* for the word *song,* and clap your hands.

    Praise Jesus with a song.
    Praise Jesus with a song.
    Hosanna! Praise the Lord!
    Praise Jesus with a song.

2. Make a tambourine. Place bells, pebbles, dried beans, or peas on a strong disposable plate. Staple another plate upside down on the first. Cover the ends of the staples with tape for safety. Have your child decorate the plates. Then shake the tambourine as you sing songs of praise to Jesus. Sing the song in Activity 1, substituting *shake* for *song*.

3. Help your child fold a sheet of green paper in half. Draw half a leaf on one side so that the fold will be the center of the leaf. Cut out the leaf just as you would cut out a heart from folded paper. Cut slits along the edges to make the sections of the palm leaves. Open the folded paper. Wave the branches as you sing the song in Activity 1. If you make ten branches, you can play the following game. First number each of the ten branches from 1 to 10. Lay the branches on the floor in order. Touch each branch as you say the matching number while saying the following rhyme:

    I praise Jesus—one, two, three.
    I praise Jesus—four, five, six.
    I praise Jesus—seven, eight, nine.
    Count to ten and praise again!

    Repeat the rhyme as long as your child remains interested.

Story Ten

1. Draw a cross about 8 inches high on paper or cardboard. Empty cereal boxes work well. Cut out the cross and have your child color it. Attach a photograph of

your child at the center. Above the photo print "Jesus." On the left side, print "Died." On the right, print "For," and under it put your child's name. Your child's room might be a good place to hang the cross.

2. Teach your child to sing the following words to the tune of "Mary Had a Little Lamb."

   Jesus gave his life for me, life for me, life for me.
   Jesus gave his life for me.
   He took my sins away.

3. Point out crosses you may have at home. Talk about and point out the crosses you see at church. Most crosses are empty. This reminds us that Jesus is no longer dead. He came back to life! He has power over death and will raise us to life in heaven.

Story Eleven

1. Try this action play with your child:

   The angel rolled the stone away.
   (pretend to roll stone)
   Jesus is alive!

   The women saw the Lord that day.
   (point out excitedly)
   Jesus is alive!

   You and I are happy to know,
   (point to smiling face)
   Jesus is alive!

   Let's tell others wherever we go,
   (walk in place)
   Jesus is alive!

2. Cut out two paper eggs of the same size for your child. Tape them together so that they open like an egg-shaped book. Have your child color and decorate the top egg. Talk about how the bright colors of eggs and flowers make us think of the brightness when Jesus rose and the new life he had. Open the book and print "Jesus rose from the dead" inside.

3. Sing the alphabet (A,B,C) song with your child. Then teach the following song to the same tune:

   Jesus came alive for me.
   Oh, how happy I can be.
   Someday heaven I will see.
   I will live there happily.
   I know that the Lord loves me.
   I will serve him willingly.

Story Twelve

1. Remind your child that Jesus is with us even though we cannot see him. Have your child close his or her eyes. Ask, "Can you see Dad? Mom? Open your eyes. Now can you see Dad? Mom? Close your eyes again. Can you see Jesus? Open your eyes. Can you see Jesus? We cannot see him, but he is with us and can see us. Someday Jesus will come back to earth. We will see him. He will take us to live with him in heaven."

2. Teach your child the following words to the tune of "Mary Had a Little Lamb."

   Friends met Jesus on a hill, on a hill, on a hill.
   Friends met Jesus on a hill.
   He rose into the sky.

   He was covered by a cloud, by a cloud, by a cloud.
   He was covered by a cloud.
   Someday he'll come again.

3. Help your child act out the story. Here are ideas! Make a hill in a sandbox or in dirt. Add a few branches for trees. Place many small objects in or on the sand (dirt) to represent people. Use pennies, buttons, crayons, pencils, buttons, or craft sticks (with faces drawn on them). Have one item be Jesus. As he ascends, cover him with cotton to represent the cloud. You could sing the song from Activity 2 as you act out the story.

4. Point out the blessing the pastor gives at the end of the church service. He raises his arms and sends us on our way, reminding us that the Lord is always with us.